Stradivari's
Singing Violin

by Catherine Deverell
illustrations by Andrea Shine

Carolrhoda Books, Inc. / Minneapolis

To my father, a barn-dance fiddler
— C.D.

To my grandfathers, Olaf Hofstad
and Aleksandrs Abolins. With thanks
to John Rieger, Airis, Gary, and
Jane Chaleff.
— A.S.

Special thanks to Julie Elhard for sharing
her expertise in early European music

This book is available in two editions:
Library binding by Carolrhoda Books, Inc.
Soft cover by First Avenue Editions
241 First Avenue North
Minneapolis, MN 55401

Deverell, Catherine.
   Stradivari's singing violin / by Catherine Deverell ;
illustrations by Andrea Shine.
      p.   cm.
   Summary: A fictionalized childhood biography of the famous
violinmaker.
   ISBN 0-87614-732-5 (lib. bdg.)
   ISBN 0-87614-583-7 (pbk.)
   1. Stradivari, Antonio, d. 1737—Juvenile fiction.
[1. Stradivari, Antonio, d. 1737—Fiction. 2. Violinmakers—
Fiction. 3. Musicians—Fiction.] I. Shine, Andrea, ill.
II. title.
PZ7.D49735St   1992
[E]—dc20   91-40395
                                                             CIP
                                                             AC

Manufactured in the United States of America

1 2 3 4 5 6 7 8 9 10 01 00 99 98 97 96 95 94 93 92

Author's Note

I must have been standing behind the barn door when musical talent was being handed out. I have never had an ear for music, and all the other members of my large family could play one or more instruments.

I can remember the tap-tap-tapping of my oldest brother's feet as he bellowed out notes on his accordian—strictly by ear. My mother chorded along on the banjo while the rest of the family played the drums, clarinet, saxophone, and organ. They were all led by my father, bowing his fiddle.

It would have been wrong to have called my father a violinist, for he was no more than a barn-dance fiddler. Yet his versions of "Turkey in the Straw" and "Comin' Round the Mountain" have never been equaled. His most prized possession was a violin he had gotten through a clever horse trade. Inside the instrument was a label that read "Stradivarius 1732."

This label gave the violin an air of mystery that all the family, except Dad, wanted solved. He would not let his fiddle be taken from our home for an evaluation.

After his death, we had the violin checked to see if it was a real Stradivarius. It was a fake. But the label itself still held a mystery for me: Who was Antonio Stradivari, the man responsible for the famous Stradivarius violin?

I soon found that very little is known of this famous violinmaker's childhood. My unanswered questions led to this book. *Stradivari's Singing Violin* is based on the few dates and facts that are known.

I believe Dad would have been pleased.

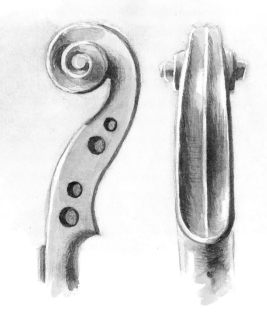

he sweet sounds of a violin
concerto floated through the air.
The cook baking bread in the kitchen
stopped to listen.

The maid making beds
in an upstairs bedroom
stopped to listen.
Children playing in the shaded courtyard
stopped to listen.

All along the street,
eager listeners
opened their windows wide
to hear the beautiful music.

Little Antonio Stradivari
was playing his violin.

Papa Stradivari beamed and bragged.

"That's my son.

Someday he will be a great concert soloist

in the royal courts."

Mama Stradivari smiled proudly.

"That's my bambino.

Someday he will be a great composer.

All the famous maestros in the world

will want to play his music."

They did not know Antonio's secret.

He did not want to be

a violinist in the royal courts.

He did not want to be

a famous composer.

He had other plans. . . .

In the 17th-century city of Cremona
(in what is now northern Italy),
the name "Stradivari"
was well known and respected.
For hundreds of years,
a saying had been whispered
in Cremona's shops and homes—
"Rich as Stradivari."
Antonio's parents,
Alessandro and Anna,
gave their children only the best.
When their fourth and
youngest son, Antonio,
had shown interest in the violin,
they had hired the finest music
teacher in Cremona for him.

Now their son was 10 years old,
and the Stradivaris believed
he played the violin
as well as anyone they knew.
But one day Antonio drew the bow
across the strings.
He stopped.
He frowned.

"What's wrong, my little bambino?"
asked Mama.

"Why are you frowning?" asked Papa.

"The sound is wrong," pouted Antonio.

"The tone is not deep enough."

"Antonio, you silly boy," smiled Mama.

"It's perfect."

"My goodness," laughed Papa.

"That violin was made by Nicolò Amati.
There are no finer violins
in all of Europe."

Papa and Mama knew
the name "Amati" well.
The Amati name had been
linked with violinmaking
for more than a hundred years.
Nicolò Amati had followed
in the footsteps
of his father and grandfather.
Papa and Mama could not believe
their young son was questioning
the work of the greatest
violinmaker of their time.
"Perhaps the violin could be tuned
differently," suggested Antonio.
Papa and Mama smiled knowingly.
They knew the music dancing
from the violin could be no better.

Later in the day,
they found Antonio taking
all the strings off of his violin.
"What are you doing, Antonio?"
asked Mama.
She was not smiling.

"Young man," said Papa angrily,
"do you think you know more
than the great Amati?
If indeed the violin should
have been tuned differently,
you should have waited
for a master's help."
Antonio did not answer.

He was too busy
replacing the strings.
Slowly he turned each key,
pulling the strings tight.
He plucked each string,
listening to their sounds.
Then he drew the bow
across them all.
The sounds were still not right.
He turned one key this way
and another that way.
He drew the bow across
the strings again.
Finally he smiled.
"There, that sounds much better,"
he said delightedly,
and he began to play the opening
to one of Monteverdi's operas.

"I do believe the tone is fuller,"
said Papa, surprised.
"Never have I heard such
perfect pitch," said Mama proudly.
"My bambino is a genius!"
The clear, sweet melody
brought tears to her eyes.

"I know what we will do,"
said Mama Stradivari,
dabbing the tears away.
"Antonio must give a concert."
Immediately she started planning
for the gala event.
She invited all their noble relatives.
She invited all their wealthy friends.
But most importantly of all,
she invited Nicolò Amati.

The day of the party arrived.
Most of the guests were seated.
Would the great Amati come?

As Antonio played his violin,
the people sat spellbound,
their hearts fluttering with joy.
Antonio finished his final concerto
to the sound of thundering applause.

"Magnifico!" shouted Amati,
coming through the back gate.
"Never have I heard such lovely
sounds coming from one of
my instruments—and played
by someone so young!"

"It was not difficult," said Antonio,
"after I tuned it to my liking."
"Excellent!" cried Amati.
"All violinists must learn to tune
their own instruments."
"Still," said Antonio, "there are
sounds singing in my head,
and I cannot make them come true
with this violin."
"Then perhaps you should learn
the trade so someday you can design
a violin of your own," suggested Amati.
Antonio beamed with excitement.
Was his dream about to come true?

"Amati is always looking for
a hard worker," said Amati.
"You may come to learn from me."
Antonio ran to his father.
"Please, Papa," he begged, "making violins
is my heart's desire."
"Well, Antonio," said Papa, "you are at
the age when it's time to learn a trade.
If violinmaking is your choice,
then how better to learn
than from the master himself."
Antonio hugged his father.
Then the boy looked up at the master.

"What if the violin were longer?"
Antonio questioned the great Amati.
Amati turned to the guests.
"Already the boy is making plans.
That *is* good.
Maybe someday the student will be
more famous than the teacher."
Amati laughed heartily at such a joke.

So while other boys of 11 and 12
were studying the verses of Virgil
or learning to cut stone,
Antonio Stradivari went to work
in the studio of Amati.
It did not take Antonio long to learn
that making a violin was no easy task.
He learned to cut and carve,
bend and sand,
varnish and polish.
Over and over,
he did the same things.
"Will I ever get past
these tedious tasks?" he wondered.

Little by little, though,
as Antonio grew older,
Amati let him place the pattern
on the wood.
He helped the boy chisel out
the delicate hole for sound,
shaped like an *f*.
He watched Antonio mix the varnish
with this much resin
and that much oil.

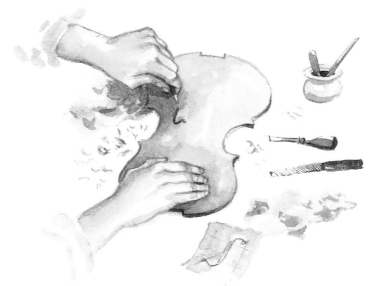

By the time Antonio was 16,
he was able to make a violin
completely on his own—
a violin that Amati knew
no other hands had touched.
Amati then let Antonio put a label
inside the violin that read:
"Alumnus Nicolaii Amati,"
which means "Student of Nicolò Amati."

But Antonio was not yet satisfied.
He could not get his violins
to play the sounds singing in his head.
So he went to his teacher
with his problem.
"I still have not been able to make
the perfect violin," said Antonio.
"Can you help me?"
"You do not make a perfect violin
at first," answered Amati.
"It takes years of hard work.
No matter how good each
instrument may seem to you,
the next violin you make will be better.
But you have learned much.
You have proven to be
my most talented pupil."

Antonio was honored by such praise.
His teacher's words never
left his thoughts.
Each time Antonio finished an
instrument, he would say to himself,
"It is good, but it could be better."

For years and years, Antonio Stradivari
worked in the shop of Nicolò Amati.
In the evenings, after Amati
and the others had gone home,
Antonio would stay to work
and to experiment by himself.
He was happiest when he was alone.
He could then get the true feeling
of the instrument's tone and quality.
Questions spun in his head
as he worked.
Which feature was the most important
in making a violin?
What was the secret to a
rich and vibrating tone?

Should the violin be longer?
Or shorter?
What about the wood?
Was maple the best?
Or pine?

And what of the varnish?
Perhaps he should experiment
with Amati's recipe, Antonio thought.
But these ideas could wait.
For the time being,
he would take the advice of his teacher.

One evening,

when Antonio was 23 years old,

Amati returned to his shop after dinner.

He stood in the moonlight

outside the studio,

listening to the high notes of a violin

floating in the still night air.

The tone was richer than any

he had ever heard.

Excitedly,

Amati burst through the door.

"It has happened!"

"The student is as good
as the teacher!" cried Amati.
"This cannot be," said Antonio humbly,
his heart racing with joy.
"But it's true," answered Amati.
"You are becoming a master at your trade.
No longer are you making
the violins of Amati.
You are making
the violins of Stradivari.
My name must be struck from your labels,
and you must be given full credit."

From that day on,
the labels inside Antonio's violins
were marked with the stamp of his initials
and his name in Latin:
Antonius Stradivarius Cremonensis
(which means Antonio Stradivari
from Cremona).
Antonio had finally made
a violin that could play
the sounds singing in his head.

Afterword

The earliest-known violin that bears only Stradivari's name was made in 1667. This first Stradivarius was different from Amati's violins, but only in small ways.

After Stradivari left Amati's studio, his violins changed more and more. He was always experimenting. His violins (as well as his violas and cellos) kept getting better and better, their sounds sweeter and deeper.

Stradivari's violins are thought to be the best ever made. Many concert violinists use them (if they are lucky enough to have one). The secret of what makes the tone of Stradivari's violins so superb has never been uncovered. Many believe it is in the varnish—how it was mixed, applied, and dried. Stradivari never wrote down his recipe for violinmaking, and no one has ever been able to copy it.

Over his lifetime, from 1644 to 1737, Stradivari made more than 1,100 violins. His finest instruments were made between 1700 and 1720, a time known as his "Golden Period." In the last year of his life, he made his final violin, which is now called "The Swan." Its label reads *"D'Anni 93,"* which means 93 years old.

About 635 of Stradivari's violins, 17 of his violas, and 60 of his cellos are still in use. Three hundred of these famous instruments belong to Americans. One such violin, the "Betts," can be seen in the Library of Congress, in Washington, D.C.

As for the missing violins, no one knows. Certainly after more than 300 years, many have been lost or destroyed. And yet, with a grand stroke of luck, perhaps another will be found (maybe hidden away in grandfather's attic).